Montessori at Home Guide

A SHORT GUIDE TO A PRATICAL MONTES-
SORI HOMESCHOOL FOR CHILDREN AGES
2 TO 6

A. M. Sterling

Sterling Production
LEXINGTON, KENTUCKY

Sterling Production
www.sterlingproduction.com
ashleyandmitch@sterlingproduction.com

Montessori at Home Guide: A Short Guide to a Practical Montessori Homeschool for Children Ages 2 to 6
A. M. Sterling – 2nd ed.
ISBN-13: 978-1512297935
SBN-10: 1512297933

Contents

i

Dedication to daughter, Nova.

"Children are human beings to whom respect is due, superior to us by reason of their innocence and of the greater possibilities of their future."
- DR. MARIA MONTESSORI

CHAPTER ONE

Introduction

Chances are if you are reading this book that you, like me, are the parent of a young primary child between the ages of two and six. Perhaps you aren't a parent, but instead a caretaker or someone who has a young person who is near and dear to your heart. You have most likely heard of many methods and styles of education, ranging from a traditional public school routine to children who have been home-schooled. You realize that at some point in the near future, decisions will need to be made about your own child's education. If you are like me, you look at your child and see eyes filled with wonder and excitement. This child seems to have more curiosity than could ever be satisfied through traditional educational methods, a child eager to go forth into the world and experience it all in their own way. You may be interested in Montessori home schooling because you see the uniqueness in the Montessori technique and you feel that it best compliments the uniqueness of your own child. Whether this is your reason, or you have another, you and your child are about to begin a beautiful, enriching, and colorful journey together.

While attending college for a teaching degree in special education, I had the opportunity to meet many incredible people. In particular, there was one boy with autism whose demeanor was very impressive, and looking back, I believe that was due to his upbringing in Montessori. Through my studies, Montessori came up more than once, but I didn't give it much thought until my husband and I had our own children. Our first child, Nova, was born in 2012 and, like any good parents we knew that we wanted to give her the best of everything, including education. Now, the research began. Together, we visited website after website, searching for the right educational technique to help our beautiful little girl achieve her true potential when again, we stumbled upon Montessori. This time it sunk in. We read everything we could get our hands on about Montessori, including posts on the bloggers' sites that you will find mentioned throughout this book. Our daughter, who is now 4 years old, has done so well with Montessori that with our newly arrived son, Mars, we would simply choose no other way to educate him. We've worked hard to understand and implement Maria Montessori's teachings in our home, and wrote this book as an easy to understand guide for other parents to do the same.

As you read on, keep in mind that one of the most beautiful things about Montessori instruction is its adaptability. If you feel that your child would benefit from a slightly different approach than ours, then by all means honor your child. I have not been able to include every piece of equipment or every activity. What I have included is some of the basics that we have found to be most beneficial for our own children. I am a mother and an educator passing on to you some of what I hope will enrich your lives as much as it has enriched mine. Congratulations on discovering Montessori! It truly is one of the most amazing and effective philosophies for educating young children in the modern world.

"As soon as children find something that interests them they lose their instability and learn to concentrate."
- DR. MARIA MONTESSORI

CHAPTER TWO

A Short History of the Montessori Method

The world of Montessori education is one in which the child leads their own experience, gently guided by an observant parent or educator. The Montessori method, developed by Dr. Maria Montessori in 1907, has become an effective and cherished lifestyle, and method of education, for children of all ages across the globe. Dr. Montessori recognized the natural rhythms in the learning habits of young children while she was focusing on how educational techniques could be improved for children with educational and developmental disabilities. She saw that if those natural rhythms were honored that the child would flourish. She opened the first children's home school in Rome over one hundred years ago. Since then her philosophies have caught on worldwide and there are now tens of thousands of Montessori schools across the globe.

The fact that there are entire schools devoted to Montessori instruction does not mean that Montessori techniques can only be practiced in an institution. In fact, Montessori philosophies are among some of the easiest to implement in your home based on how natural they are to your young child. All that you really need to begin your Montessori home school is an understanding of the basic Montessori principles. At the most basic level, Dr. Maria Montessori recognized the following principles as being essential to the development of the young child:

- Movement and use of the senses is closely related to cognition and understanding.
- Even the youngest of children thrive when they are allowed to maintain some control over their own lives. A child that is given some choice in their education is more likely to comprehend and retain the information learned.
- Young children, as well as adults, learn better when they are engaged in an activity that they enjoy. By providing children with activities that they enjoy and find stimulating, a love of learning is fostered.
- External rewards such as certificates and trophies do not supply the same amount of satisfaction as self-respect and a sense of pride. For these reasons, awards for behavior and accomplishments should be limited.
- Learning is best done when the environment makes sense in terms of what is being learned. This point alone makes Montessori perfect for the home environment.
- We learn from each other.
- How the educator interacts with the child influences the outcome. The educator, or parent in this case, is more of a guide or director rather than an authoritative figure.

- Everything has a place. That includes physical objects as well as our thoughts. When a child works in a clean, clear environment that makes sense to their activity, they are better able to retain and properly store the knowledge gained.

As you can see, so much of Montessori is about respect for the mind and spirit of the child. As a parent, no one is more capable of loving, respecting and honoring your child than you are. You are the perfect Montessori educator for your child.

"If teaching is to be effective with young children, it must assist them to advance on the way to independence."
- DR. MARIA MONTESSORI

CHAPTER THREE

Montessori Homeschool Environment

The first task to take on once you have made the decision to incorporate a Montessori lifestyle into your home school is setting up the environment. This need not be a daunting or expensive task. In fact, creating your Montessori home school can be done very simply by utilizing many items that you probably already have and creating routines that are inherently natural to your child. As you create this world for your toddler or young child, stop and think about what the world looks like to them. A major focus of the Montessori method is the fostering of independence and building of life skills at an early age. Most importantly, a Montessori home school offers a comforting, safe place for growth. Be gentle not only with your children, but also yourself as you embrace these new routines. If you are new to Montessori, there will be lessons for you to learn as well as for your child. Take this opportunity to grow together as a family and enjoy watching your children blossom. Anastasia, a Montessori mother and blogger at montessorinature.com, describes the Montessori home perfectly:

> *"A Montessori home has space for mistakes, it offers peaceful and quiet time to observe, explore, make independent choices and support when needed."*

Following are some simple ideas that will help you prepare your home, and establish routines to start you out in the wonderful world of Montessori.

Bringing it Down to Earth:

If you have little ones in your home, and I am assuming that you do since you are reading this book, you have probably spent some time on the floor with them, playing and interacting. This lower space is where your child spends almost all of their time. You have probably spent time and energy making sure that the space is safe for your child. This is extremely important since you want your young child to have safe, unencumbered access to their world. Most parents think very carefully about which items to put up out of reach, and those items, which can cause harm, should be placed out of reach. However, for a moment get down on the floor with your child and think about what might be missing from their environment. How would you feel if the world around you looked so big and inaccessible? To start your young child in a Montessori environment, you will want to give them access to as much as possible, as safely as possible. Bring these items to their physical level as much as you can. For instance, if you have a tall bookcase in your home make sure that all of your child's books are on shelves that they can reach, or better yet add a shorter bookcase to the room. Three shelve bookcases are relatively inexpensive and can house a variety of your child's books, toys and supplies. Add a sense of reality to it by taking some family photos down from higher places on the walls and placing them on the lower bookshelf. Consider adding flowers or other real decorative accessories. This will help your child to feel as though they are part of your entire home. It also provides an opportunity to teach your child how to care for and respect the items in your home.

Consider all of the items your child uses in your home on a daily basis, and think about how you can help your child be more self-sufficient when using them. It isn't always possible to rearrange things, but you can make accommodations. For example, rather than lifting your child up to brush their teeth, provide a stool in the bathroom along with making sure all of the supplies are within reach. Add a small countertop mirror, so that they can watch themselves and consider purchasing faucet attachments that extend the handles so that they may be reached easier. Keep a small basket of pillows and blankets in the living room rather than the linen closet, so that if your child wishes to cuddle up, they have access. Teach them how to fold and return the blankets to the basket when they are done. These items may not be what you immediately think of when you hear the word education. However, small changes like these will make a big impact in the daily life of your child. As you adjust yourself and start to make these changes, you will begin to notice more opportunities for bringing the world within your child's reach.

Get Rid of the Clutter

As a homeschooling parent, I have been guilty of letting the clutter accumulate. It is easy to do when your home is the center of daily learning. Books, papers and supplies pile up; toys are played with all day and are spread through every room, sometimes the household chores have to take a back seat. I also recognize that I am my best in a clear, clutter-free environment. It should come as no surprise that children also thrive in uncluttered spaces. Take a look at your child's surroundings from their eye level. Are there items piled into the lower spaces of your home, such as small tables, lower shelves, bottom drawers, under the furniture, etc.? It is time to clear out as much as possible or develop a different storage system, if possible. Young children have short attention spans and become easily distracted. A clean, clear environment allows them to better focus and concentrate on what is important. If you are finding that the clutter seems to be focused around your child, then this is a wonderful opportunity for introducing the importance of accountability in taking care of their things. Make clean up as easy as possible for them by having designated places for their toys, clothes, books, etc. This is a perfect time to teach them to put one thing away before getting out another. A Montessori home is one where everyone is involved and children thrive on the pride of being able to take care of their own things.

Keep it Real

Many parents who choose Montessori for their children do so in part because of the focus on real life play and learning activities. Creativity is the act of using the imagination. For young minds, the best creativity comes from interaction with reality. When possible choose real, everyday items for your child's play. For example, if you have a child that loves having tea parties, choose a real tea set complete with utensils and linens over a plastic child's tea set. Let your child use real pots and pans in their kitchen play, complete with a small tub of soapy water to wash the dishes in, or give them real musical instruments, rather than play plastic ones that sound nothing like the real thing. This will help encourage creativity long after your child has outgrown his or her toys. This can be a difficult adjustment for many families to make. You may be worried about breakage or incorrect use. Think of this as an opportunity to teach your child that accidents happen, and how to prevent them. Evaluate your child's toys and decide if there is a more realistic version that they could use instead. As you begin developing your Montessori activities, you will find yourself using everyday items in a variety of ways, and you will notice for yourself how your child's creativity grows with the most ordinary of items. You do not need to feel like you have to eliminate all of your child's fantastical play items. There is no need to take away any cherished possessions, or discourage their use. However, when cleaning out toys or considering the purchase of new ones, you might want to ask yourself these questions:

I.   Will this toy foster my child's interests and provide pleasure?

II. Is this toy somehow based in reality, does it make sense to the young mind?

III. Will this toy encourage creativity or hinder it? Is the purpose too limited?

Having toys and activities based in reality may seem a little boring at first. Take a moment to think about a princess dress-up kit. A child can spend endless time role-playing a character, and they will have many experiences while role-playing, but ultimately, their play goes no further than being a princess. If on the other hand, the child was provided some sparkly material, and maybe a stick and ribbon to make a wand, they first have to imagine these items being turned into a princess costume, then they have to use reasoning to build it. Once the princess play is finished, they will likely find other uses for the material. This slight change of perspective can have a large impact on the creative development of your child.

Set Up the Space

While a Montessori home school can include as much of your home as you wish, you may also want a designated space for some educational activities. With a child in the 2-6 year-old age range, you will find that many learning opportunities will not be limited to certain rooms. Children this age are curious; they move around often and have short attention spans. Daily interaction is their primary method of learning. However, this is also the perfect age to introduce a special learning space. Consider your long term plans for home schooling when creating this space. Are you planning to only

home school through the preschool years or do you see yourself home educating further into the future? It is also fine if you are not sure yet. You might want to begin with a small area of your home. This could be anything from a small corner "workstation" in your living area, to an entire designated room. For younger children, you really do not need that much space to start your Montessori home school, and setting up a small work area to begin with will save you from feeling overwhelmed, and extra expense. You need just a few basic items to set up a workspace. First, you need a child-sized table and chairs. This is extremely important. Your child needs a workspace that makes sense and fits the size of their bodies. You will also require a low bookshelf to keep activities and supplies on. Baskets, bins and trays are also very handy for keeping items separate and making clean up easier and more natural for the young child. We like to purchase baking sheets from the Dollar Store for our activities...cheap yet functional! Here is a list of items to consider when building your workspace.

Essentials:

- Child-size table
- Child-sized chairs, one for each of your children and at least one or two more for guests
- A low bookcase or cubicle. Your child should be able to easily see and reach anything on top of this piece of furniture. IKEA is a fantastic place to pick up things like this!
- Age appropriate items for chosen Montessori activities. A more detailed list of activities and supplies will be provided later in the book.
- Several rubber storage containers or other storage devices.

These do not need to remain in your schooling area; in fact it is recommended that they be removed. You will want to give your child a limited choice of several activities in their workspace, and have the supplies accessible to them. You will likely have many activities that you want to try or a supply of materials that do not fit the current activity choices. Since too many choices and too much clutter will over-stimulate the young mind, you will want a place to store your materials until they are ready to be rotated into use.

Helpful Items:

- Extra bins, baskets and trays.
- Colorful, realistic, stimulating decorations for the area.
- A work rug.

Of course there are plenty of additional items that you may add to the workspace, depending on your available space, needs and finances. One thing to keep in mind when creating a workspace is that the area should be as simplified and uncluttered as possible. Make sure everything has a reason. Some decorations and wall art not only add character to the space, but can also stimulate conversation and creativity. There is a difference between carefully chosen pieces and just adding randomness to the space. Make sure that the space makes sense to your child.

Daily Routine:

Children, especially young children, require a predictable routine. This is vitally important to establish as you begin home schooling your child, regardless of the method of education. The daily routine will help establish security, boundaries and self-confidence. Each family will have its own daily rhythms, as will each individual child. A Montessori home school environment is one in which those naturally occurring rhythms are honored. I personally like Sindy's philosophy regarding daily routine and order from www.youtube.com/whynotmontessori:

> *"Habits such as order and consistency in presentations aid our children to better master their aptitude and accuracy. Daily, one must remember to observe and respect our children by not interrupting their concentration. Encouraging our children's contribution to the life of the family or other social groups is also suggested (cleaning, table setting, pet care, etc.)."*

For a child as young as 2 or 3 years of age, plan on no more than one to two hours of scheduled educational activities. This does not prohibit you and your child from participating in more, it simply acknowledges the limits of children that young. An older child of 5 or 6 years of age will likely be able to handle up to four hours of activity time. Remember also that since you are doing Montessori at home, that learning and growth activities will be a part of your day well past scheduled instructional time. Your daily schedule should also include regular daily activities such as self-care and clean up.

To begin designing your routine and setting a schedule, first think about the practicality. Consider what time your child wakes, how long they take to eat breakfast, fight off grogginess and prepare for the day. Allow time in your morning routine for your young child to take care of himself. It may save time to brush their teeth for them and get them dressed, but allowing them to learn to do these things for themselves fosters independence and self-reliance. Perhaps you feel that instructional time will be best spent later in the day. Make a list of all of the things that must be done before focusing on instructional time. Allow your child to help with as much of the list as possible.

Young children have short attention spans and will require frequent breaks and changes in activities. Do not plan for one or two activities to take up several hours. A good rule is to plan on thirty to forty-five minutes per activity depending on the age of the child. A two year-old will likely require your assistance in helping them focus for any length of time, while a six year-old will be able to work independently for that same amount of time. Break up activities with shorter periods of about ten to fifteen minutes of story or circle time. Circle time is a concept used in many Montessori classrooms and it can be effectively used in a home school environment, even with only one child. Have a designated circle, or space for your child to sit in between activities. This can be utilized as a way to center and focus the child before the next activity. Use this time to read a story or talk, either about what they just did or an entirely different subject. Remember that your daily routine should be one that honors both you and your child. This may take some time to figure out, and will likely require periods of adjustment as well as trial and error. Even once you feel that you have a solid routine in place, you will find that as your child grows and develops that your daily activities will need to be adjusted. Following is a sample Montessori home school routine.

8:00 a.m.: Wake up, use bathroom, get dressed

8:30 a.m.: Prepare/eat breakfast, clean up

9:00-9:15 a.m.: First circle time

9:15-9:45 a.m.: Activity time

9:45-10:00 a.m.: Short story or song/dance

10:00-10:15 a.m.: Circle time

10:15-10:30 a.m.: Snack time

10:30-11:00 a.m.: Activity time

11:00-11:15 a.m.: Short story or song/dance

11:15-12:00 p.m.: Activity time

12:00-12:15 p.m.: Clean up

12:15-12:30 p.m.: Final circle time

12:30 -1:00 p.m.: Lunch

1:00-2:00 p.m.: Free play

What is important to notice here is not the exact times or durations, as those will vary with each family, but rather the rhythm that is in place. There is a clear start to the day; a routine that is always followed, then educational time is started with circle time. The child understands that this first circle time marks the beginning of the instructional period. Clear breaks allow the child to transition from one activity to the next. By having a set number of activities before breaks such as snack time, your child begins to understand the concept of time. Eventually, this will become so second nature even to the youngest child that they will begin to transition by themselves. Allow for a range in flexibility in your routine. The exact minutes on the clock do not matter as much as the rhythm. If your child is losing interest in his or her self-directed activity ten minutes early, you may try to keep them interested a bit longer. However, it is acceptable to acknowledge that your child has gained all that they require from that lesson today and it is time to move on to the next phase. The same is true for extending activities. There is no need to interrupt a child that is engrossed in discovery. Simply let the interest and curiosity be satisfied in its own time and then carry on with the day. This is the beauty of Montessori home school, being able to tailor the experience to each child. Marie, from www.childledlife.com describes her personal experience of how to best accommodate the child's natural schedule in the Montessori home school environment:

"We like to create a prepared environment, but do not require participation at a specific time. We have a dedicated learning classroom and choose to spend a specific amount of time in the mornings each day. Lessons come from the interest of the children. We notice their curiosity and create lessons around those interests. It helps to keep 2-6 year olds interested because THEY choose when and what they will learn. Other times of the day are open play in a prepared home. We also keep busy by taking advantage of free community events like library story time and church bible studies."

Montessori is a combination of concepts that come naturally and those that take effort to commit. If you are reading this, you have likely already learned at least the basics of Montessori concepts, and decided that it seems like a good fit for your child. For some the most difficult task is changing the mindset. Montessori can be infused throughout your entire day, and the focus on self-reliance contradicts much of what we see in modern parenting techniques that focus more on doing things for the child. Immerse yourself at your own pace. You will be a more effective Montessori educator and parent if you allow the mindset to develop at its own pace rather than forcing it all at once. Each day, attempt to add in one more Montessori aspect. Let your three year-old set the table, ask your two year-old for help sorting socks and build a routine one hour at a time if you need to. Just like any other lifestyle change, creating a Montessori home will require patience, dedication and persistence.

"It is through appropriate work and activities that the character of the child is transformed. Work influences his development in the same way that food revives the vigor of a starving man. We observe that a child occupied with matters that awaken his interest seems to blossom, to expand, evincing undreamed of character traits; his abilities give him great satisfaction, and he smiles with a sweet and joyous smile."
- DR. MARIA MONTESSORI

CHAPTER FOUR

Essentials for the Montessori Home

Your Montessori home school can be as basic or abundantly stocked as you desire. Within this method you have the freedom to choose what you will use, create and invest in, depending on your needs, desires and budget. There are of course, items that are essential, but even those have options. Many Montessori tools can be handmade, or created from things you already have in your home. As you read through this list, it is important to not feel overwhelmed. You do not need everything at once, and some things you may choose to never use at all. Matt from www.montessorimatt.com offers this great advice concerning Montessori supplies:

> "If I had to pick "must have" items, I would say invest in the golden beads and stamp games. You can do almost any math with those. As far as what is in the home, remember Montessori is more a philosophy dealing with the normal development of the child. It helps the child master his or her environment. Your house is probably full of things they can learn to master."

The following list is a sample of supplies for use by children ages 2 to 6 years of age in the Montessori home. Many of these items are

 practical, and will be of use for years to come. Durable Montessori materials will serve you well into the future.

For the Surroundings: As we discussed earlier, there are some essential items for setting up a Montessori environment. These objects will make it so that all things are accessible to your child, as well as provide ample space and freedom of movement in the work area. Items in this list include furniture pieces as well as items that contribute to the overall atmosphere:

- Child-sized table and chairs.
- Storage baskets and bins that can be labeled.
- Work/play rug.
- Low-level bookcases/shelves.
- Small lamp that is easily turned on and off.
- Child-sized comfortable reading chair, if budget and space permit.
- Assortment of books.
- Household decorations such as photos in frames, art, statues, mirrors, etc.

Basic Activity Supplies: Regardless of what activities your child will be participating in, there are some general supplies that you should always have on hand.

- Pencils, pens, markers, chalk, etc.
- Art supplies such as paint, glue, beads, etc.
- Paper, paper and more paper of all kinds.
- Self-care and cleaning supplies, such as hand soap and paper towels.
- Trays or baking sheets. These will be used to as portable workstations for each activity.
- Place mats, or another type of work mat.
- Small scoops, tongs and tweezers.
- Cups or muffin trays to be used for sorting activities or keeping supplies separate.

Everyday Household Items: Much of what Montessori is for this young age group is learning self-care and self-reliance through the proper use of everyday household items. Marie from www.childledlife.com offers this advice when it comes to what everyday items to include in your routines and activities:

"We have taught our children to use most things as their own. With training anything can be used. Adult size scissors, paring knives for preparing food, and full size forks. Children want to follow our lead and will request to use items they see us using. Another must have in a home is a space for children to have their own plates, bowls, utensils, and cups in the kitchen. We store ours in a low kitchen drawer, but a cabinet would work just fine."

Some items from your home that you might consider your child having access to include.

- Cheese grater. A good starting activity for a four or five year-old is grating bars of soap.
- Real scissors. Children's safety scissors are often clumsy to handle and can be difficult to maneuver. Teaching a child to cut with pointed scissors allows them to more quickly master fine motor skills.
- Utensils for cutting soft fruit and a cutting board. Make sure they are not too sharp, but not so dull that they are ineffective. Always supervise your child.
- Pots and pans, dishes, etc. for pretend play.
- Cleaning supplies such as a gentle vinegar and water (50/50) cleaning solution, sponges, dish soap, towels, short broom, dust pan, etc.

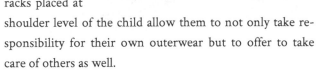

- Plants for daily care.
- Coat hanging racks placed at shoulder level of the child allow them to not only take responsibility for their own outerwear but to offer to take care of others as well.
- Sturdy, non-skid step stool or a handy learning tower (the one in the picture actually folds for easy storage!).
- Accessible linens, including those that can be used for play.

Encourage your child to make their own bed, even if it might be a bit messy by your standards. Always keep a few towels and washcloths where they can reach them as needed. A big basket that holds a few blankets and pillows allows a child to take some responsibility for their own level of comfort.

This list is by no means all-inclusive, nor are you required to use what is on it. The point is to take a look around your home and think about ways to implement many of your own household items into your routine. It is also meant to point out that even the youngest of children are often ready for a bit more responsibility than we give them credit for.

Sensory Development

Pink Tower: The pink tower is a set of 10 pink cubes that increase in size from 1 cm3 to 10 cm3. There are several very specific exercises that you can use the pink tower for, the purpose of which is to fine tune visual discrimination of dimensions as well as improving fine motor skills. The pink tower is also an excellent introduction into mathematics and will be able to be used in additional activities as the child ages.

Cylinder Blocks: These are long wooden blocks, with removable cylinder pieces of varying and increasing sizes. Each block resembles a puzzle, with holes cut out in which to place each cylinder. The cylinders have small knobs on the top of them by which they should be handled. Similar to the pink tower, the cylinder block teaches visual discrimination of sizes and is an introduction to early mathematics. The fine motor skills involved in handling the knobs in each cylinder help prepare the child to correctly hold writing instruments.

Red Rods: A red rod set includes 10 rods, ranging from ten centimeters to one hundred centimeters in length. Each rod is exactly ten centimeters longer than the next smallest. Along with being used for specific activities, children are drawn to red rods for imaginative play as well. Red rod activities encourage the development of fine motor skills, visual discrimination of sizes and introduce mathematics.

Touch Boards: Usually presented in a set of three, each of these small boards is divided into a section of either two five or ten. Each section has a different tactile finish. The child uses the sense of touch to complete various activities. Touch boards are good for all children in the two to six year range, however younger children and those with sensory disabilities will gain the most from their use. Touch boards develop tactile sense and can prepare the child for the movements involved in writing.

Mathematical Development

Spindle Boxes: This is a long wooden open top box that is divided into ten sections. Each section is clearly numbered 0-9. Along with the box, a set of spindles is included. There are several activities that can be completed with a spindle box, however the simplest and most widely used is number recognition through placing the correct number of spindles into each corresponding slot. Spindle boxes are excellent for young children to visually recognize numbers and introduce an association between the written number and quantity. Since zero is also included, the concept of none is also introduced.

Sandpaper Numbers: These are small green boards with a sandpaper number placed on each. These provide an introduction to numbers and sequence that is also reinforced by tactile sensation.

Number Rods: These rods are very similar to the red rods mentioned in the sensory section. The sizes and increments are exactly the same. The main difference is that number rods alternate in colors between red and blue. The shortest number rod will be blue, the one that is ten centimeters longer will be red, next one blue, and so on. These rods, which are visually divided into ten centimeter sections help the young child learn to count, recognize relationships between numbers and begin to visually grasp the concept of quantity.

*Please note that the materials included in the mathematical section are just the basics to start out with and are meant for the very young child. If you have a child that easily grasps the concepts presented you may be ready to introduce more advanced materials, which have not been discussed here.

Language Development

Sandpaper Letters: Similar to the sandpaper numbers described in the mathematics section, sandpaper letters are letters of the alphabet that have been stenciled or traced, cut out and placed onto small boards. A red and blue background scheme is used to differentiate between vowels and consonants. These help the child develop language sense through a tactile experience with a visual element as

well.

Moveable Alphabet: This is a complete set of both upper and lower case alphabet in movable pieces, with a visual color distinction between consonants and vowels. Vowels are blue and consonants are red. These are used to help prepare the child for reading, writing and transferring the auditory word into a visual representation.

Phonetic Object Box: This is a very useful Montessori tool, and it is one that really requires little to no investment. This is a box with different items, usually twelve, placed into it. Depending on your child's age and skill level, the items in the box should be easily decoded phonetically, such as cup, pen and car. I find that a shoebox, labeled with the letter of study, works perfectly for this. You will work with your child to help them develop a sense of phonetic awareness.

Other Language Supplies: Language is one of the areas that actually require very few resources. You will want plenty of level appropriate books, paper, index cards, folders, and if possible a reading station in the work area. There are almost countless activities that can be created from these simple items alone.

Practical Life Development

Rather than include a list of items you could buy for this area of child development, I feel it is more important to go over a few of the skills your child can master. Most of these require absolutely nothing in terms of additional equipment. Through practical life exercises, your child will gain confidence, self-sufficiency and the ability to properly interact with others in their world. The focus of practical life activities should be how to care for themselves and their environment, as well as safely maneuvering through it. Think along the lines of proper hand washing, dressing oneself, opening a door, carrying scissors, watering a plant, taking care of their workspace, etiquette, etc. We will later discuss a few specific activities for practical life, however you will be presented with countless opportunities throughout the day that require no planning, but rather a keen eye to acknowledge them as they occur.

""The environment must be rich in motives, which lend interest to activity and invite the child to conduct his own experiences."
- DR. MARIA MONTESSORI

CHAPTER FIVE

Montessori and Your Child Ages 2 to 6

As an observant parent, you have noticed the miraculous development that has occurred in your young child. In just a few short years, your child has developed from a helpless infant to a person capable of logic and complex thought. While your young child is still honing in on these skills, there is no other period in their life where so much cognitive growth will take place. By embracing Montessori in your home, you are further encouraging your child's development by respecting and honoring the natural growth process that is taking place.

Children at this age learn best by experiencing through their senses. Their attention spans are too short to sit through lengthy instruction. They have not yet developed the reasoning skills to benefit from lecture, and while their language skills are developing, they are nowhere near the point where they can learn entirely from printed instruction. This leaves the wide world of their senses. This is how we learn and adapt, as infants, and young children are still very much still tuned into these natural instincts. Anastasia from www.montessorinature.com makes the point with her statement:

"I believe that in the Montessori environment children learn through using their 5 senses and working with their hands. It is important to supply children with materials that allow self-correction, develop fine motor skills, represent reality (e.g. book with realistic characters), and encourage diversity."

Montessori allows children to experience and learn from the world through these pathways. Most Montessori activities are purposefully created to allow learning to be reinforced by some sort of sensory experience, even if at first it doesn't seem completely obvious. This is the subtle beauty of many of these activities. Reinforcement is taking place without needing to be pointed out.

For most children, there is a pretty clear lineage of cognitive development. One thing naturally occurs before the other. Unfortunately, as parents we are often presented with timetables that tell us exactly when we should expect to see such development. While the tables certainly prove to be a useful tool in recognizing developmental delays, it is important to recognize your child as an individual. Not every child will fit perfectly into a time slot of development. As a Montessori parent and educator, you will honor where your child is at this very moment, and not worry about where they should be. Children of this age will naturally be curious about what they don't know. They will also become bored when a task is fully mastered. By allowing the child some freedom in picking between several activities, you are giving him or her opportunity to self-select their areas of growth. Of course, some activities will be considered more fun than others. Occasionally an activity may seem too challenging and a child may become discouraged from choosing that particular activity on his or her own. As the parent, it is your responsibility to recognize the readiness cues of your child. If one activity is performed with speed and ease, then it is time to remove that activity from the rotation and provide an alternative that offers a bit more challenge. The opposite is true when you see your child struggling. You do not want to foster an attitude of "This is too hard, I can't do it", but you also do not want to inhibit or discourage learning in any way. If you see your child having trouble, sit with them and help guide them through. Do this repeatedly for the activity time, if necessary. Do not force, but gently encourage. If you find that your child is unresponsive, then it is time to consider removing the activity and replacing it with another. As you read through some of the following activities, you will notice that most activities focus on multiple skills. Often you will have several choices when helping your child learn a new task or skill. Perhaps number rods provoke no response in your child, but they love the spindle blocks. The concepts of counting, number recognition and quantity association can be taught using both. Again, it is important to recognize your child's readiness and not let the structure of what someone else says they should be doing dictate their process. Matt from www.montessorimatt.com offers a great example of how he chooses to let the child lead:

> "Take some pressure off (of) you. They do not have to be interested in what you made or prepared. They might be later if not now, but just wait and see what the child is interested in. I have a 3-year old student right now in my class. He seemed uninterested in everything he did except when he looked at books. I used that interest to show him the sandpaper letters, then pointed out different letters in the books he was reading. Take what they love and find connections to the environment."

Choose the method that works for your child until they are ready to move on to something different.

Have you ever noticed that your young child seems like a sponge? Every little thing you say or do is closely observed, remembered and sometimes copied. This is the stage of human cognitive development that all areas of the brain are the most open and receptive to new information. Perhaps you have heard that you should introduce a new language to your young child, or about the importance of reading daily with them. This is because, at this point, your child's knowledge is not yet solidified. The area of the brain that controls language development does not yet recognize restrictions. It is simply trying to absorb all the words, meanings and dialect that it can. As we mature, we become more certain in what we know. At times, this contradicts with things we want to learn. This of course is much more complicated than I am presenting here, but the point is that at this age, your child is an open book. You will want to take advantage of every opportunity to expose them to as many new concepts and experiences as possible. Allow them as many sensory experiences as they are capable of handling. Your child is excellent at cueing you in on when they have had enough. If you go out for a nature walk, stop and compare the difference between standing in the sun and in the shade. Have your child smell various flowers and plants. Let them feel the different textures of trees and leaves. Try to differentiate between birdcalls, etc. There is opportunity in any activity for exploration and growth.

"Respect all the reasonable forms of activity in which the child en-gages and try to understand them."
- DR. MARIA MONTESSORI

CHAPTER SIX

Activities

Now let's focus on specific Montessori activities that you and your child can participate in during your school time. Remember that there are so many possibilities for learning activities, and that those suggested only represent a few. Over time you and your child will develop your own favorites and adaptations. When you find the activities that speak to you, do not feel that you should push them aside in favor of something more traditional.

My daughter loves anything that has to do with art. Painting, drawing, and coloring can be used to teach so many different subjects, for example painting letters and numbers.

For Sindy from www.youtube.com/whynotmontessori, her favorite activities for a 2-6 year old would be "working with the sound cylinders, sandpaper numerals, meal preparation and all astronomy-related lessons." There is great variation among families. Learn to honor these differences and your child's unique interests.

If times or ages are mentioned in any activity, please take that as a guideline only. Children will learn the activity as it comes naturally to them. A thirty minute activity may take your child forty minutes. If the suggested age is four, but you have a three year old that can grasp the concepts do not let the recommendations hinder you. This information has not been provided for all activities. This is for a couple of reasons. One being that some of these activities span broader age ranges. The other is that while I find that sometimes it is useful to have an idea of where to start your child, it is better to look at your child in terms of ability and readiness rather than number of years. If times are included, they are meant for assistance in planning your day only. They are not in any way intended to be a marker for your child's success. The activities have been divided up into the instructional areas of language, mathematics, sensory development and practical life skills. Many of these activities can serve as crossovers, allowing you to introduce multiple concepts at once. Some subjects such as cultural studies or science are included in practical life skills, since at this age that is primarily what those subjects encompass. Where applicable, additional skill areas have been included at the end of the paragraph for your reference. For the sake of simplicity, activities have not been listed more than once.

Language Development Activities

Object and Sound Comparison: From around your home gather a selection of items that your child is very familiar with and can name. These can either be household items or play toys. Depending on your child's level, decide if you want to focus on beginning, middle or ending sounds and choose items that offer a variety in those sounds. For instance, if your child has a collection of toy animals, choose a cow, pig, sheep, dog and horse. You may also choose to incorporate movable alphabet parts or sandpaper letters if you wish. Have your child spread the animals and letters, if you are using them,

out on a workspace, such as a tray. Talk to your child and demonstrate letter sounds, making sure that your child is watching your mouth as you speak. Have your child repeat the sounds with you. Once you feel ready, ask your child which objects begins with a certain sound. For a younger child you could make the "P" sound and ask which animal begins with that sound. An older child may be able to associate the letter form with the sound and the object. If your child is having trouble picking the correct object, assist them by having them slowly say the name of each item with you again and asking them if they recognize the "P" sound in any of them. Your child will use a combination of auditory, visual and tactile senses to reinforce this activity. This activity is suitable for ages 2-6, as you can focus on different sound placement, and a variety of phonics. The introduction of sandpaper letters or the movable alphabet is better suited to the older child.

Sandpaper Letters: The letter blocks are easy to make if you would rather not invest in a premade set. Simply trace and cut out the entire alphabet on pieces of sandpaper. Each letter should be a few inches in height. Make sure that the script that you use is consistent throughout, and that you stick to either upper or lower case letters. Once you have the letters cut out, adhere them to small boards of a contrasting color. Most Montessori schools prefer to start out with lower-case cursive.

Keep the sandpaper letter blocks face down when you put them away. Allow your child to gather several letter blocks, without looking at the letter side of them. For a young child, no more than three or four should be practiced at a time. Sit with your child, and working with one board at a time, turn it over and talk about the letter. Name the letter and make the letter sound. Do this until your child can begin to replicate you. Discuss together what words begin with that sound. Next, your child will practice "writing" the letter. Take your child's index finger, and trace it around the shape in the same direction that you would use when writing the letter. Let your child experience the movement of forming the letter. Finish by letting the child demonstrate the knowledge that they have learned during the session.

You can extend this activity by having your child write letters using their fingers in various tactile substances such as sand or shaving cream.

I. This activity is for the child that is just beginning to recognize letter sounds and the associated images.

II. This activity can also be used for sensory development.

Movable Alphabet Word Formation: While it is possible to use a simple set of refrigerator magnets for this activity, it is advised that you either purchase or make a special set of the moveable alphabet, with one color designated for consonants, and the other for vowels. The color differentiation helps the child to recognize the different roles of the letters. A set of refrigerator magnets contains too many colors to add this benefit. It is also nice to have more than one complete set, so that as your child's word-building skills develop, he or she will be able to compose longer words and phrases without being limited to the contents of one copy of the alphabet. Store these letters in a compartmentalized container that separates the letters. This helps making finding the correct letters easy, and also provides additional opportunities at clean up time.

To begin the activity, choose a set of words for your child to work with. Typically short words that follow the consonant-vowel-consonant rule are good to begin with. Each sound is easily recognizable and there is minimal blending to confuse the child. Word families work well for this type of activity also. The words mat; cat, rat, sat and hat all belong to one word family. The words car, far, bar, and tar belong to another.

Once you have chosen a small group of words begin by demonstrating to your child how you make words by listening to the sounds and choosing the correct visual representation to go along with it. Make a word for your child, going through each sound step by step. For the next word, allow your child to lead and help them work through it if they hit a difficult spot. Continue, letting your child independently attempt to build words.

i.   This activity is usually for children ages 4-6, who have a solid recognition of letters and are beginning a grasp on letter sounds. Work on this activity for no longer than thirty to forty minutes.

Chalk Letter Writing: Sometimes, Montessori activities are so simple that they seem almost too obvious. When you encounter activities such as these, take a moment to think about in what other ways your child's educational experience can be enriched by participating in the activity. An example of this is chalk letter writing. Using a small chalkboard, you are going to have the child begin writing letters. You will want to work on only one or two letters at a time. For this activity you will need a sample letter for the child to copy. Sandpaper letters work great for this activity as well, since they are slightly larger and provide an additional tactile experience.

Have your child sit at the table with the sandpaper letter in close proximity to the chalkboard, preferably directly above it. Before beginning to write, reinforce the letter name and have the child trace the letter with their finger repeatedly in the same direction that they will be writing the letter. Next have your child write the letter on the chalkboard as many times as they would like. They will need to be responsible for cleaning their board as it fills up. Provide the child with the proper cleaning materials and show them very specifically how to wipe the board. Demonstrate the up, down and side to side motions to thoroughly erase the board as opposed to haphazard swishes with an eraser that leave distracting streaks.

I.   This activity can be continued for as long as desired, however keep an eye on the child to ensure that they are staying on task and not getting distracted by random doodling.

II.   This activity can also be used for sensory development and practical life skills.

Phonetic Sound Box: This is an activity using the phonetic sound box that is aimed toward the older child that is getting closer to independent reading. Find several items from around your home that have short spellings with sounds that can be easily decoded. For example: pen, tag, cup, dot, etc. Once you have collected the items, create index cards with each item spelled out in clear letters. Let your child randomly pick a card and help them read it. First see if he or she is able to recognize the sounds, and then offer assistance if needed. Ask the child to make all of the sounds on the paper and then attempt to find the item with corresponding sounds from the phonetic sound box. Continue by repeating the exercise with the remaining cards.

I.   As with most activities that require more concentration, pay attention to the cues from your child in regards to how much time to spend on this activity. Thirty minutes is a good timeframe to stick with, however if you notice that your child seems to be growing tired or frustrated, begin leading the activity to close.

Mathematical Development Activities

Sandpaper Numbers: Nearly identical in presentation to the sandpaper letters used above, sandpaper numbers will show your child how to properly form numbers, along with reinforcing the name of each visual representation. The numbers used should be zero to nine, however zero should not be introduced until the child has had an opportunity to learn and understand the concept of none.

This seems pretty basic, however to a young child that is associating order and quantity to a visual number, it can be difficult to grasp the concept of nothingness.

Present the numbers to your child, one at a time. Have them trace each number with their finger, in the same direction that they would use when writing, while practicing saying the name of each number. Present the numbers in logical order. Depending on the age of the child you may be able to present multiple numbers in one session, or you may be limited to the presentation of one number at a time. You can take this activity further by using the chalkboard to practice writing numbers in the same way that it was used to write letters.

I.   This activity is intended for the younger child, or ones just beginning number recognition.

Spindle Box: For this activity you will require a spindle box and a complete set of spindles. This is also one of those pieces of equipment that can easily be created if you do not wish to purchase one. All you need is a long box, with enough dividers to separate the box into compartments numbered zero through nine. You will also need enough small rods for the child to place the appropriate number into each slot.

Sit your child down and count with them from one to nine, while pointing to the numbers on the box. Include zero if your child has already been introduced. If not, you may want to wait until the spindle part of the exercise before including zero.

Once you have gone through the numbers, demonstrate putting the correct number of spindles into each slot. Point to the number one, say the number and pick up one spindle and drop it in. Assist the child with the number two if necessary and allow them to continue according to their skill level. Once you have completed the entire box, point out the zero slot to the child. Illustrate that there are not any spindles in the box because the number is zero and zero means none. Ask your child to explain zero back to you if they are capable. If not, be sure to reinforce the concept of zero in each spindle box activity until they have a firm grasp on it.

Number Rods: Number rods are excellent for introducing a variety of mathematical concepts, and are a great investment for your Montessori home school as you will have continued use of this product for at least a couple of years. A good number rod set will include instructions for several activities, the most basic of which is a simple ordering exercise that will help introduce the concept of the rods to your child. Begin by spreading the rods out onto a work surface. For this particular part of the exercise, it is best to begin with a tray or mat that is positioned horizontally. Ask your child to find the shortest rod and place it on the tray, next to it have the child place the next largest and continue until all pieces have been placed and you can visually see the progression. Each number rod is divided into one-centimeter cubes, with each rod being one centimeter longer than the last. Count the marked squares on each rod. Illustrating how one cube is shorter than two, two is shorter than three, etc. The combination verbal and visual reinforcement will help to solidify the concepts of order and quantity recognition. You can also do the reverse by starting with the longest rod and graduating down to the smallest.

I.   The visual sorting of number rods by length can be done by a child as young as two years old. A child will need to at least have a beginning concept of counting to perform this entire activity as is.

Sensory Development Activities

The Pink Tower: The pink tower is a series of pink cubes that gradually increase in size in all dimensions; length, width and height. The blocks themselves are very smooth. The goal of the pink tower is to teach visual discrimination between sizes, and also to practice some specific fine motor skills by handling the blocks one particular way.

Have the child arrange the cubes randomly on their work area, such as a table or mat. Demonstrate to the child how you will be building a tower starting with the largest cube on the bottom and the smallest on top. Next demonstrate proper handling of the cubes. Each cube should be held on the top with only the thumb and the index finger, used in a gripping fashion on opposite sides. As the cube is lifted, the opposite hand should slide under the cube, providing a base for the cube to be carried on. The cube is then transported with the support of both hands. It is not that these cubes are unusually heavy or difficult to manipulate. The handling activities are in place to emphasize care in handling objects and fine motor growth. The actual tower will be built a few feet away from the work area, requiring the child to maneuver between the two stations. In addition to transporting the cubes, the child will have to figure out the next sized cube without the previous one right next to it for comparison. This of course can be modified for a younger child, where the cubes are placed in order on the work space before transporting to build. Have the child place each new cube as directly in the center of the previous one as possible. This illustrates balance and stability.

When it comes time to complete the exercise, have the child dismantle the cube tower in the same fashion that it was created, returning the cubes to their original home in the same arrangement that they were in to begin with.

I. This activity can be used for a range of ages as it teaches several concepts.

II. This activity can also be used as a mathematical development exercise.

Cylinder Blocks: This activity can be done using one set of cylinder blocks, or multiple ones depending on your child's level and your supplies.

To use a cylinder block for a younger child, begin by demonstrating how to remove each cylinder from the block. On top of each cylinder is a small knob. The child is to grab the small knob with the thumb and index finger, in a pincher type grasp. The cylinder is then removed by lifting up on the knob. Once the cylinder is removed, place the cylinder near the block, in front of the hole that it just came out of. Repeat with each of the remaining cylinders. Once all of the cylinders have been removed, let the child look into the holes so that they begin to visually recognized space and how it is filled. One by one have the child replace the cylinders in the same manner that they were removed.

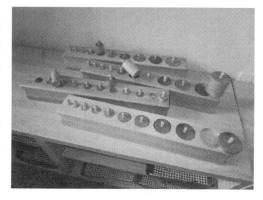

A slightly more advanced child can use just one block, but confuse the placement of the cylinders once they have been removed. This encourages them to use spatial recognition to choose the best option for each cylinder to be placed back into. This activity can be taken even further with the use of multiple cylinder blocks.

I. This exercise can suit a wide range of age and levels.

II. This activity can also be used for mathematical development.

Tactile Touch Tablets: For this activity you will need to either purchase touch tablets or create your own using small boards that are exactly the same size and about three different textures of sandpaper. You will make two boards of each texture, by covering an area of the board with the sandpaper. Make sure that the boards you create are identical in shape and coverage.

Have your child bring the tablets to their workstation, and have the child feel the difference in each board. Ask them questions like which is smoother and rougher, and if any of them feel the same as another one. Once you have introduced the textures, use a soft blindfold to cover your child's eyes. Ask the child to feel each board and determine which ones match each other.

I. This activity can be used for a range of ages. It is an excellent activity for calming a hyperactive child. The careful focus on texture, combined with the quiet blindfolding helps to center and refocus the child.

Mystery Grab Bag: You will need a solid cloth bag that is large enough to hold several items and has an opening that your child's hand can easily fit into. A drawstring bag is ideal but it is not a requirement. Choose multiple items from around your home of varying shapes and textures. Try to have good contrast in the items. For instance, a craft pom-pom, metal spoon, rubber ball, feather, wooden yo-yo, etc.

You can begin the activity by putting your hand into the bag, grab an object and without taking the item out, describe it in as much detail as possible. Use words that describe texture and shape. Ask your child if they have any ideas of what the item could be. Pretend that you do not know and take guesses yourself. Next for your child's turn have them do the same thing. Encourage them to use as many words as possible and to take guesses as to what the object might be. Once the item is revealed, talk to your child about features of the object and use the opportunity to introduce new vocabulary.

I.   This activity is for a range of ages, and actually makes a fun family game if everyone contributes several mystery items.

II.   This activity teaches vocabulary and encourages imagery to recognize and describe various objects.

Practical Life Activities

This is the area where you will find so many opportunities that it seems to be almost a disservice to attempt to narrow it down to a few select activities. Instead, this section will point out many daily opportunities to practice life skills. The activities listed will not have detailed descriptions because many of them are self-explanatory by just the title alone. You may use this list to recognize moments that you can teach life skills. You can also use this list to choose specific life skill activities to add into your work time. I recommend choosing at least one of these to focus on each week. Let these skills build upon each other by continually reinforcing learned skills while providing the opportunity to learn new ones. When demonstrating life skills, it is important to remember that each of us has our own unique way of doing things. While certain techniques should be mastered, for example doing a button, your child should not have to do their buttons in the same order that you do. It is perfectly fine if you start at the bottom and your child starts in the middle. Keep this in mind as you teach these skills. Learn to recognize the specific things that must be taught, such as safety. However, allow your child the room to go and develop their own best method. You will find that the young child will better retain skills and information if it comes naturally to him or her, rather than a rehearsed action meant to mimic exactly what you have demonstrated.

Adapting Into Society: In our world there are unspoken social rules that we abide by in order to be successful and happy. These activities should focus on demonstrating to your child how to practice social etiquette, courtesy and respect.

Specific behaviors to demonstrate include appropriate daily interactions such as greetings, introductions, saying thank you and excuse me, how to give and accept a compliment, when to show respect and allow others to go first, assisting people in need, answering a phone, how to wait in line, offering to take someone's jacket, and how to properly interrupt a conversation.

Also focus on activities that involve personal hygiene, such as covering your mouth for a cough or a yawn, excusing oneself to use the restroom, making sure hands are clean before offering to shake hands with someone, etc.

Daily Self Care: Children this age love to do things for themselves, and it is encouraged to allow them to do so whenever it is appropriate. Demonstrate simple dressing techniques such as how to maneuver buttons, snaps, zippers, ties, buckles and other closures. Show your child how to put on sock correctly and how to fasten or tie their own shoes as their motor skills mature. Teach them how to take care of their own dirty clothes when they change them.

A young child should be given the opportunity to brush their own teeth and wash their own body, face and hair with your supervision. Proper hand washing technique is one of the most valuable life skill activities that you can teach your child.

Home Care: The young child relishes the opportunity to mimic your activities and feel like they are helping you. Indulge this natural desire and teach them important life skills at the same time. Fill your child in on your regular cleaning routine and let them help where appropriate. They will begin to gain an understanding of the importance of this work as well as a respect for the time involved. Suitable activities for a child this age include laundry sorting, folding and putting away, helping to load and unload a dish washer, washing dishes by hand, polishing furniture, sweeping, counter wiping, watering plants, and setting the table.

Everyday Motor Skills: Often times these activities are overlooked because they seem so natural and commonplace. However, to a small child, these tasks can be somewhat daunting. If you have ever watched a child struggle to open a door or shakily carry a glass, then you understand that even these most basic of skills need to be demonstrated and practiced. Help your child in these areas by taking the time to notice the obstacles that they encounter throughout the day. Some opportunities may include properly pulling out a chair from a table, locking/unlocking a door, pouring a beverage, opening containers that are both hard and soft, hanging up coats, dusting off shoes, folding clothes, opening closets, making a bed, changing the toilet paper roll, turning lights on and off, and countless more. Take every opportunity that you can to help your child make his way in the world.

Cultural Awareness Development: When we really stop to think about it, there is practically endless opportunity to introduce our children to other cultures and their traditions. This is vitally important in helping your child become an aware person. These activities do not need to be elaborate. It can be anything from a meal prepared out of regional ingredients to a simple ceremony. As an example, Anastasia from www.montessorinature.com uses this activity:

> "My favorite activities I have incorporated in the past were activities that replicate cultural traditions of different countries. For example, when learning about Japan tea ceremony, children were offered an

activity on the shelf with two cups, some ice tea in a pot and a mat. Two children could work on this activity. They placed a mat on the floor, served each other a cup of tea, set on their knees in front of each other, and enjoyed their tea together."

Take this opportunity to also learn as a family. There is an enormous, beautiful world out there with so much richness and diversity to explore.

"Of all things love is the most potent."
\- DR. MARIA MONTESSORI

The Happy Montessori Home: Key Points to Remember to Help You and Your Child Stay on Task and Succeed

At certain points, especially as you are starting out on your Montessori journey, you may feel overwhelmed and at times even like things are out of control. There is a lot of freedom in Montessori instruction. If you and your family are accustomed to more rigid routines, this may be a difficult adjustment in the beginning. Following is a set of a few simple rules that will make your home schooling day easier and more effective for both you and your child. A major point of frustration for Montessori home schooling parents is how very hard it can be at times to keep the child on task. With the freedom to choose activities comes the desire to start and stop as they wish. Montessori work areas are full of fun potential, and the young wandering mind may find it difficult to focus at times. Sitting with your child and forcing them to do a certain activity until you are satisfied with the outcome defeats the Montessori practice to a certain point. This does not mean that you are helpless in getting your child to focus and remain on task. The following points should be given respect in any Montessori home school, however if you are finding yourself frustrated with a fluttering child, make an extra effort to enforce these policies:

First and foremost, the child must have respect for the materials in the learning environment. Each item has a purpose in the space. Unless you are encouraging imaginative play during free-play time, it is important that the child understand that each object is only to be used for the designated activity. Your child will have free choice of activities. If they choose an activity, they use the materials properly. All materials must be returned and cleaned up when finished. Rather than focusing on punishment for improper behavior, teach that actions have consequences. If your child likes activities that use the pink tower, but mostly because they like to throw the cubes at the wall, it is time to teach the child that the pink tower is no longer an option until they are able to respect the cubes and use them properly.

All work must be done in a designated area. Most Montessori educators use some form of a work space. This can be a table, floor mat, tray, etc. Once the space has been designated and an activity has been selected, the activity should not move from that space. All work needs to be completed in that area. The designated work space allows for a clean area that focuses only on the task at hand. By combining work spaces, or allowing a child to move from one work space to another, you are encouraging distraction. Staying in a work area can be especially challenging for younger children. Sit with the child if need be until they get accustomed to completing each activity in one space.

If you have more than one child in your Montessori home school each child is not allowed to intrude upon the work of another. This means no sharing of work, no interrupting of work, no interfering with another's workspace, etc. Your child needs to learn respect for another's process and space. If a young child is especially excited about their own activity it can be difficult to get them to temporarily contain their excitement. However, this is a vital lesson to teach. We cannot interfere with another's work because we are excited about our own. Each child must respect the other's work.

Along with not intruding upon another's work is learning to not touch the work of another child without expressed permission from the creator of the work. If one child does not want to share their own work, this is completely acceptable. It helps to teach autonomy and independence of thought. It also provides the opportunity to witness how their decisions about their own possessions can affect others.

Accountability is key. The child should have the responsibility to clean up and return each work station to the condition that it was in when they found it before moving on to the next activity. If you have a child that likes to jump from one thing to another, being consistent on clean up routines can help to curb some of that extra energy. Realizing that they have a responsibility to clean up first, rather than just going on to the next activity will help them make decisions about the rewards of actually finishing the chosen activity. Oftentimes, a complete activity is easier to clean up than one that is in mid progress. For younger children teaching accountability takes repeated effort and patience.

Also, don't forget to look within yourself. Young children are often mirrors of us. If you are stressed, tense or are taking more of a dictator type role in your Montessori environment, you will have different results. Think about your role and how you are presenting yourself and the educational philosophies to your child. Sindy from www.youtube.com/whynotmontessori says:

> "Observation is key. As a teacher/guide we must put an emphasis on learning rather than teaching, our primary role is observing the child and providing an environment for him based on our observations. By following the child, his interests and sensitive periods, we'll be able to adequately provide activities a 2-6 year old can keep engaged in. During presentations/work time, silence and concentration are a priority; we should eliminate distractions even if one must use a minimum of words and movement. Finally, we must allow 2-6 year old children the freedom to explore and grow at their own pace, all while embodying patience ourselves."

If you are having difficulties, think for a moment if you are providing a quiet, respectful, model for your child. This all takes time to learn. Be gentle on yourself during the process, and think about Marie's words from www.childledlife.com:

"I feel understanding and patience is a key element of a Montessori home. Many parents and home care teachers do not have formal Montessori training and can get frustrated when lessons don't go as described in books and articles. Understand it takes time to help children learn proper Montessori techniques and it takes patience to let children learn in their own time."

Finally, you know your child better than anyone else. If you are having a very difficult time keeping your child on task, stop and consider if they are in fact ready for the activity, or if they have just been at it for too long that day. Consider how your child acts when not engaged in Montessori educational activities. Do you feel that there is a larger behavioral issue to address, or is this something that can be handled simply by adhering to a few rules? Any home schooling parent that is being honest will tell you that there are days, weeks, even months that seem to be a struggle. At some points you may doubt yourself and your ability to be your child's educator. This is all completely normal. The rewarding part is when you make it through these periods, when you see how the Montessori activities that you have chosen have enriched your child and fostered an amazing love of learning. You and your child will develop a mutual respect for each other, and with persistence and love you will reap beautiful rewards. Maria Montessori recognized this over one hundred years ago, and now you have the opportunity to experience as well.

Best wishes to you and your family as you start out on this wonderful journey.

Read the previous book in the "Montessori at Home Guide" series, "A Short Introduction to Maria Montessori and a Practical Guide to Apply her Inspiration at Home for Children 0 – 2".

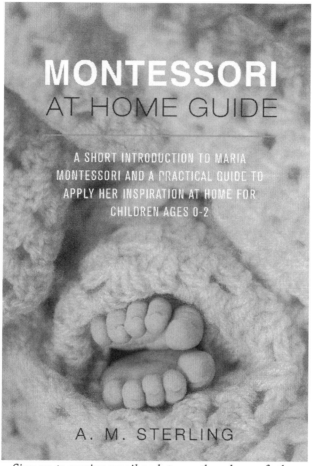

MONTESSORI
AT HOME GUIDE

A SHORT INTRODUCTION TO MARIA MONTESSORI AND A PRACTICAL GUIDE TO APPLY HER INSPIRATION AT HOME FOR CHILDREN AGES 0-2

A. M. STERLING

Sign up to receive email updates on the release of other books in the "Montessori at Home Guide" series here: http://www.sterlingproduction.com.

Resources

For More Information About Montessori Education and Inspiring Ideas and Stories, Check Out These Wonderful People:

Anastasia at
montessorinature.com

Matt at
montessorimatt.com

Marie at
childledlife.com

Sindy at
youtube.com/whynotmontessori

Additional Resources

www.montessori.org
www.amshq.org/Montessori-Education
www.montessori.edu/homeschooling.html

About the Authors

Ashley and Mitchell Sterling are new author/indie-publishers and video-bloggers on YouTube known as 'Fly by Family'. When they're not writing or talking to a camera lens, the Sterlings value their time together, in the beautiful bluegrass-laden wilderness of eastern Kentucky, where they live with their two children, Nova and Mars.

-Visit their website: www.sterlingproduction.com
-Visit them on YouTube: www.youtube.com/flybyfamily

Thank you for reading our book! We would love to hear from you in an honest review on Amazon or Goodreads!
Sincerely,
Ashley and Mitchell Sterling

Made in the USA
Charleston, SC
19 July 2016